Minor Hockey Mayhem

Memorable Moments
and
Comical Characters
We All Know and Love

Written By
Ziyad Emara
Illustrated By
Jennica Lounsbury

This book is dedicated to my Mom, Dad, and brother, each of whom provided me with constant support and helped me realize my dream of writing a book about hockey.

All moments and characters depicted in this book are simply meant to highlight the lighter side of the minor hockey experience. They are in no way meant to insult or offend anyone. Any resemblance to actual persons is purely coincidental.

Copyright © 2020 Ziyad Emara

All rights reserved. No part of this publication may be reproduced, distributed, or transmitted in any form or by any means, including photocopying, recording, or other electronic or mechanical methods, without the prior written permission of the publisher, except in the case of brief quotations embodied in critical reviews and certain other noncommercial uses permitted by copyright law.

ISBN: 978-1-7773161-0-5

This book was typeset in Kingthings Clarity by Kevin King

Since the age of five, my weekends have revolved around hockey. I recall when my parents first introduced me to the game, I would spend my time on the ice crying as I pushed along a hockey skate trainer. As time went on, I began to develop an obsession with the game and have cherished every moment spent with my teammates, friends, and coaches on and off the ice. Hockey has taught me many things: how the sting of a loss is just as valuable as the elation of a win; how as a team, we either sink together or swim together. Playing the game has helped me develop my leadership and teamwork skills; as captain, I learned that with responsibility comes humility, because it's not about being in the spotlight—the true fulfillment comes from working towards a goal as a team.

Throughout my years of hockey, I encountered several frequently-occurring moments and characters, and thought it was long overdue to put these into a book for my fellow hockey enthusiasts to enjoy. These twenty frozen-in-time moments and characters are familiar to all hockey players, Tyke to Midget, and are the subject of frequent jokes in dressing rooms.

I would like to dedicate this book to the countless volunteers, coaches, arena staff, referees, parents, grandparents, siblings, families and players who help make minor hockey such a life-changing experience. We cannot thank you enough for your hard work and dedication—this would not have been possible without you.

Sincerely,
Ziyad

A portion of the author's proceeds from this book will be donated to programs that create opportunities for all children to play hockey.

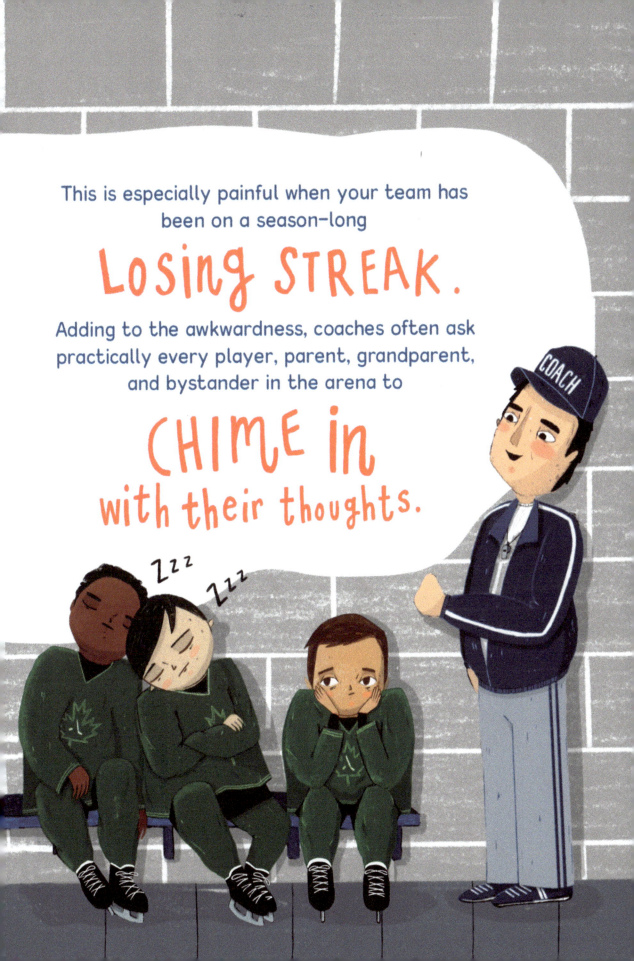

Classic Coaches

2. Botched Line Changes

Early in your hockey career, coaches are fully in charge of shift changes. Shift changes SHOULD occur when play is in the opponents' zone or when your team has secure

POSSESSION of the PUCK.

Sometimes, a well-intending coach may not realize what he or she is doing and will insist on a defensive line change at

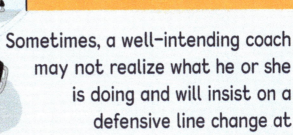
the WORST POSSIBLE MOMENT,

giving your opponents a 3-on-0 breakaway. Your poor goalie will be left

HANGING out to DRY.

Classic Coach

3. Old Yeller

Coaches constantly give commands and instructions to players, whether they're on or off the ice. Overly passionate coaches yell at the top of their lungs so every living thing in the arena with ears can hear them. Half of the time, no one can make out **A WORD THEY'RE SAYING.** Mass confusion ensues. Distracted players, who can no longer think straight, exchange awkward glances, wondering who or what is the target of the screaming.

Pregame Protocol

4. One-Inch-Per-Hour Zamboni

Before each game, the Zamboni floods the rink to provide a fresh new sheet of ice. Once players are dressed and ready for action, they wait on the bench for the Zamboni to complete its **LAST LAPS** around the rink.

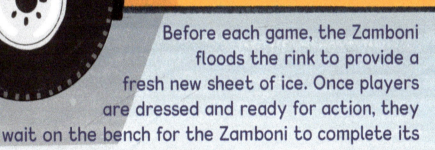

Young hockey players aren't the most patient people, especially when the Zamboni seems to drive at an inch-per-hour. By the time the ice is finally ready, it feels like you've **OUTGROWN YOUR HOCKEY GEAR.**

Pregame Protocol

≶ 5. The No-Shows ≷

To demonstrate dedication to the team, it is imperative that players show up for **PRACTICES, GAMES,** and all other **TEAM EVENTS.**

PRACTICE DAY

There's always **that ONE kid** who coincidentally is tied up and can't attend any practices, but is miraculously free on all game days.

GAME DAY

Pregame Protocol

6. Mr./Ms. Last Minute Arrival

It's important for players to arrive around thirty minutes before game time to get dressed and warm up. There are always *the rebels* who choose to conveniently show up the moment the referee blows his whistle to start the game. Adding to the delay, these late-comers tend to be *the slowest dressers on the planet.* By the time they join the game, it's halfway through the second period.

Beginner Basics

7. THE NOOB

As you grow older, you'll find fewer beginners in your division, with the atmosphere becoming more competitive. It's pretty rare to encounter a player in the Bantam division who still *doesn't know which way to hold their hockey stick.* While players want to be welcoming, it's frustrating to be stuck on a team with the beginner. With everyone getting equal ice time, the opposing team is sure to take full advantage of the newbie's shift, piling on *at least 15 goals.*

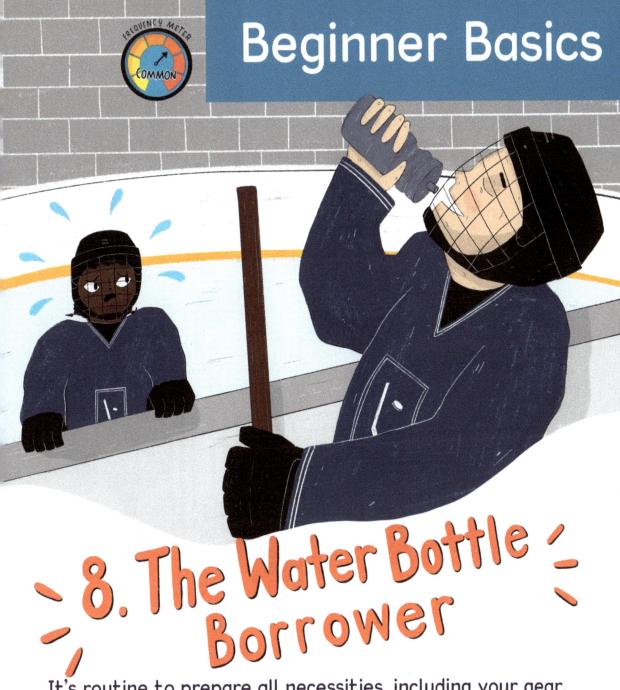

Beginner Basics

8. The Water Bottle Borrower

It's routine to prepare all necessities, including your gear, water bottle, and stick BEFORE a game. If you forget your water bottle, your teammate carries the burden of keeping BOTH of you hydrated. In a game situation, the **Victim of this DREADFUL SCENE** takes one sip of their full bottle and gets on the ice for their first shift. They return to the bench parched, only to find their **now-empty bottle tossed on the floor.**

Before each faceoff, the referee points to where the puck drop will take place. Some players are completely oblivious to this instruction and line up at the faceoff dot on the

other side of the ice.

In addition, it should be pretty obvious that the direction to skate in is TOWARDS the OPPOSING team's goalie. Then again, there are those players who still need to be reminded not to charge full force at their OWN goalie and blast the puck right into his or her mask.

Prominent Players

10. The One-Man / One-Woman Show

The only real way for your TEAM to succeed is if you play as a TEAM. Nevertheless, there's always a puck-hog that chooses to do one or more of the following: shoot the puck directly into a line of five defenders instead of passing to a wide-open teammate in front of the net; skate ten laps around the opponents' net to find a good angle to shoot from, then miss by a mile; skate from one end of the rink to the other, or coast to coast, without passing the puck.

Prominent Players

11. Mr./Ms. 24 Hour Shift

In minor hockey everyone is supposed to have equal-length shifts. There's always that one kid who thinks he or she can take all the time they want on the ice, ignoring the waving, yelling, and hollering on the bench. Their shifts tend to last **SOMEWHERE BETWEEN 1 to 2 FULL PERIODS.**

Prominent Players

12. Size Differential

It is said that size doesn't matter. But it does. In fact, size plays quite the role in swaying the progression of a game and results in serious mismatches between teams. Take the case where you have an ox and a mouse heading for a loose puck along the boards. Who do you think will get the puck? Upon "accidental" impact who do you think will be sent flying into the stands? Similar logic applies to goaltending. Massive goalies can simply maintain one position for the entire game, thus serving as an impenetrable brick wall. Tiny goalies, on the other hand, have to do an acrobatic running long jump just to get across the crease, which rarely works.

Prominent Players

13. Mr./Ms. Rage

It's essential to keep a level head in any sport, because if you lose your cool, you and your team will be penalized. Some players require more anger management than others. In their extreme forms, these hotheads might plaster you to the boards with a **BONE-CRUNCHING HIT** or swing at your head with their stick if you accidentally brush past them.

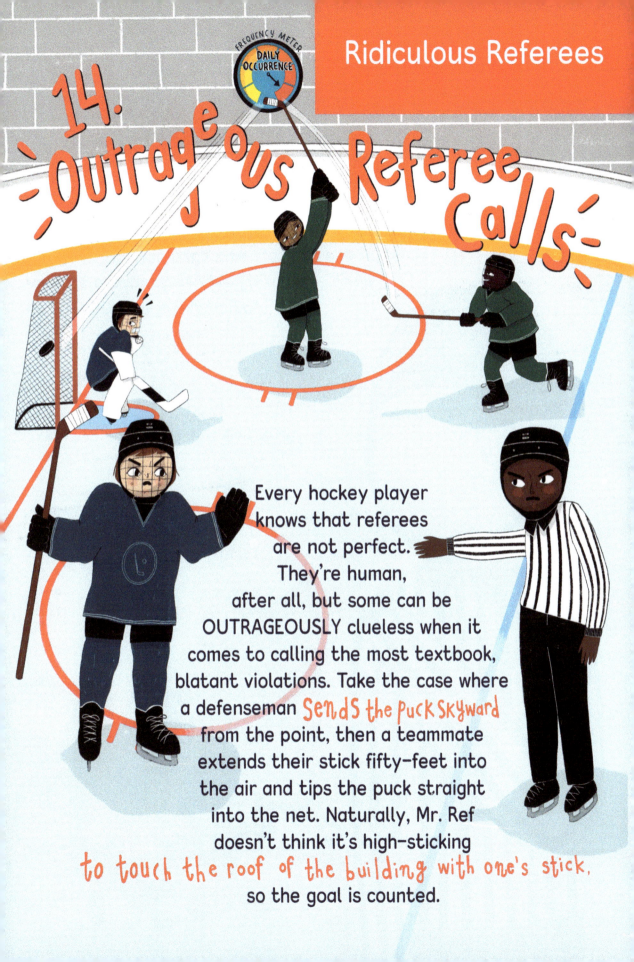

Ridiculous Referees

15. The Slooooow Whistle

Once the goalie maintains full control of the puck, a referee will typically blow their whistle. For some reason, there are refs who take eons to blow the whistle, allowing opposing players to take full advantage of this lag by **hacking away at and FLATTENING the goalie** until the whistle is finally blown.

Ridiculous Referees

16. Penalty Box Overload

At some point during the season, there's that rare spectacle where a HUGE SCUFFLE erupts on the ice between all the players on both teams. The aftermath is the referee stuffing as many players as possible into the penalty boxes with a resulting density of 3 players per cubic foot.

Fanatic Fans

17. NHL-Caliber Fan Base

Fan enthusiasm is known to have a major impact on the outcome of a game, especially for the home team. Even in Peewee, you run into teams with the rowdiest NHL-caliber fan base. Opponents always SEEM to have the louder fans. This contrast is best illustrated when an opponent successfully completes a two-foot pass, resulting in their fans giving a standing ovation, screaming at the top of their lungs, ringing 10 cowbells in unison, and erupting into an orchestra of horns, clappers, and rattles. Meanwhile, if you dangle your way through five players and score a top-shelf beauty, you'd be lucky to get a sneeze or clap of acknowledgement from your team's less-than-enthusiastic fans.

Fanatic Fans

Celebrating too early can single-handedly spoil a "big win" with seconds left in a game. Fans should NEVER assume victory and must remain calm, cool, and collected until the final buzzer, or else the opponents may very well pull off a full-scale DOUBLE-DIGIT COMEBACK.

18. The Jinxer

	1ST	2ND	3RD	TOTAL
HOME	7	5	0	12
AWAY	0	0	13	13

Terrible Teams

19. Not-so-Mercy Rule

If your team is getting smoked in a game, don't worry, the scoreboard is on your side! Proudly presenting... THE MERCY RULE! If your team is down 32-3, the scoreboard will display a face-saving score of 8-3. Why? So your spirits aren't crushed by the extreme deficit. Whoever came up with this considerate idea didn't realize that by going out of their way to make the score seem more reasonable, the frozen scoreboard actually makes it more obvious that a team is getting creamed.

Terrible Teams

20. Bottom of the Barrel

In every hockey league, including the NHL, there's always that one team that just *can't win a single game*. We've all been a part of that team, closing out the season with a record like 3-21-1. As long as you don't take it too seriously, it's pretty comical when you race home to tell your parents you only lost by fourteen goals instead of nineteen. When your team does find some way to pull off a W, especially in overtime, the celebrations tend to be of **EPIC PROPORTION**, comparable to a Game Seven victory in the Stanley Cup Finals.

About the Author

Ziyad Emara was born in Windsor, Ontario, Canada in December of 2005. He attends school in Ann Arbor, Michigan, USA and spends his time between the two cities. Ziyad has played in the Windsor Minor Hockey Association since the age of five. His hobbies include chess, photography, basketball, golf, playing piano, following the stock market, and public speaking. His dream is to give all kids the opportunity to participate in minor hockey and to encounter its memorable moments and comical characters.

CPSIA information can be obtained
at www.ICGtesting.com
Printed in the USA
BVHW090024021221
620994BV00002B/2